INTRODUCING NICKEL AS THE NEW CURRENCY.

In Yahweh God We Trust

David Gomadza

www.twofuture.world

Copyright © 2024 David Gomadza

All rights reserved.

PAPERBACK ISBN: 9798334115590

DEDICATION

A better universe linked by nickel as a universal currency

CONTENTS

TABLE OF CONTENTS
INTRODUCING NICKEL AS A NEW CURRENCY 1
FAILURE OF BITCOIN AS A CURRENCY 5
STAT 6
WHY NICKEL 7
ABOUT DAVID GOMADZA 10

ACKNOWLEDGMENTS

Tomorrow's World Order

INTRODUCING NICKEL AS A NEW CURRENCY

Nickel = 0898285898
Start value = 11000000000
Expenses = 2000000
Balance = 10998000000
Sent to bank = 10000000000
Pay all = 6000000
Balance = 992000000
Create a code for nickel
N = stuvwxyz = nickel
That means n = nickel
Symbol = n
Value = 1 US$ DOLLAR = N
Now if n =1US$ deposit in = US$ 1 = 1 value
Now if n = 1 US$ then n = n= 1
If we ask what can be of then n=1xnxn^{2}-n=n

that means that n=n-n=n-n-n-n-n-n and so on
in that regard n-n=1-1=0
that means value can drop to 1 but we will still have nickel with us
in the reserves meaning n=n for life but value could be 0
Now what can be of this nickel that other metals don't have
1. Value sometimes higher than most metals
2. But can be lower than other in value that means we can also ask what can be of nickel and know the value but could still be subjective
3. Nickel is lightest material
4. Nickel value fades slowly
5. Nickel is easy to move around than cooper etc.

Introducing Nickel As The New Currency

6. Nickel does not rust

Setting up wireless transaction for nickel

1. Ask what is nickel wireless value it is 089848382 meaning we can easily substitute value into an equation and get a code so nickel = 089848382
2. Transaction = -089848382
3. Value at end = value at start – value at end =
4. X- [-089848382] =x-n
5. Where n is the value of nickel

If we ask what can be of nickel then this is the answer value can easily be calculated over time the electronic transaction is easily stored as we can use dead humans using a simple create e.g.

Create.start.calculationsofnickel.start.preserve.memory.nameofdeadhuman.start.now.ACT

That means we can easily add everything inside that person memory forever recording all transaction and asking exactly what we want to achieve

Buy dead humans from the gods for 2 shells shells money used by angels and the gods now what to do is to ask 8 critical questions that if answered then forms the basis for the transactions

1. What is the initial value =99200000
2. What is value at start 992000000
3. What can be nickel that can be of money nickel is both physical and electronic and value might be recovered because money is lost but nickel can be returned in that when you spend then the value is spent but with nickel the value remains if we ask the correct questions then we get the correct answer so who owns nickel right now the answer is davidgomadza but with reservations because he need to state that in public and tell people where to send the nickel by post since its very light but valuable every 38 degrees is where nickel is from gold and every 48 degrees is where gold is from the north pole
4. So calculate 48 degrees of the north pole there is gold

and then 84 degrees from that place to another place clockwise then 28 degrees is the other point then calculate 18 degrees from that to the next gold perpendicular then 28 degrees at right angles then start again from the south pole the same so its anticlockwise calculate 84 degrees then 28 degrees then 18 degrees to the next gold deposit but once you find nickel then you have the worlds richest money ever because all metals will expire one day but only nickel will remain because it is the only currency that remain forever as easily derived from humans deposits and can easily be forged with less expensive equipment if we ask then this is the answer nickel will forever remain valuable even if other metals replace it but can be money again if someone wants to acquire nickel

Nickel is easily acquired by asking everyone with nickel to send it to davidgomadza now what is to be is to be because anyone with nickel becomes the most powerful after 2025 wars because nickel soon becomes valuable again but it depends now as things are changing as other circumstances come into play like bitcoin in 2026 reach saturation as it becomes expensive for anyone that no one sells and no one buys value become 1 million per each on 28 March 2026 but who can pay 1 million for a value you cant see when there is STAT new money introduced that has both value and physical appearance in material so people shift from bitcoin to this STAT to restart with hope of value quickly as bitcoin collapse on 28June 2026 as anything those who hold forever in hope of getting their value but now no one buys until I ruled it worthless in preference of a controlled currency after people have lost a lot of money with nothing to get out of this If we look at this then people revert to dependable thing so now this is the beginning of something great that means nickel can still play a big role This is what I do

1. Collect all nickel by asking for all deposits for free

since its mine
2. ask people who can forge to forge it for us
3. Ask people to buy your forged nickel to prepare to use it as cash
4. 4 automate everything by 2 shells and start

Start.nickeltransactions.start.start.transactioninnickel.start
Substitute nickel n = 08982850 and add value of 992000000 as starting capital now add value of 992000000 nickel as value at start now minus 2 shells for storage = 1000 nickel
Balance =991999000
That means balance is 991999000 today 25/07/2024 at 08:46
Yatime
We need an app that transact in nickel using YAP that means Ya.Pay what this means is that we
Ask.davidgomadzaauthorised.licensed.checkya.askya.ya can ask a few more questions
Ask.davidgomadza.create.ya.p.start
What can be of nickel that other materials can't be
2. what can be of nickel as money in the future
3.What can be of value in the future
4.What can be of money and nickel in the future that means we can ask what can be of value to us but not to others if we get nickel as currency what can that change as value in the future everything can became valuable again as nickel exchange hands on earth as well as in heaven only nickel can bridge earth and heaven in terms of money

FAILURE OF BITCOIN AS A CURRENCY

Bitcoin problems will start 26 March 2026 when it reaches a value of 1 million before collapsing on 28 June 2026.

STAT

    I am a new currency part cash part promise to pay developed to easy the pressure after the bitcoin rally in 2026 that saw bitcoin hit 1 million but instead of making people rich it bankrupted everyone in that it made it look unrealistic that something with no value can and not tangible can have value in fact can actually be worth 1 million as someone started to say people are crazy they pay 1 million for nothing where is bitcoin worth 1 million hence someone developed this currency that pays half cash and half as a promise to pay as a note that say I will pay half when I can for now complete the purchase but this kind of agreement is only possible after a crises like the bitcoin crises but I did not last as it was only meant for people to afford things at half price with the promise then written off officially hence more loses until I was replaced by nickel again dominating the world but again as just a promise as it turns out to be the new bitcoin starting at 1 US$

    0898385 is the nickel code

WHY NICKEL

Failure of the current system meant a revert to the best known and probably still the best monetary value there was and there is this is because bitcoin will rise so much that it will lose its importance for most but a few who would have collected most of it who will become rich but for a short time as they will hang on to it to increase value but at the same time will erode in intricate value as the people see no point of still trading in a shadow currency where there is no tangible benefits as a result a new global power in Tomorrow's World Order will right off bitcoin after a lot of people lost their money and court case against the owners who will come out then will make them disappear forever hence the need for a trusted currency that will see most of the people benefit from it in that nickel has value we need to just collect all from the earth for the value to increase exponentially this is how things are intended so we can say that bitcoin played a role for humans to realize how nickel can be a currency again after centuries out of play the financial crises associated with bitcoin in 2026 means the need for a new currency that can make people trust the monetary system again this is the only way forward because the reason why people are running to bitcoin is with issues with the current money system where money is simply printed from paper they use as toilet paper as well that alone means no future and value in human currency hence the need for a mineral bases monetary system that takes all this into account as said before money will become the issue in 2026 hence we must act fast and put things in place before the crises unfold hence the introduction of nickel as the new currency

BACKGROUND TO NICKEL

Nickel is a chemical element; it has symbol Ni and atomic number 28. It is a silvery-white lustrous metal with a slight golden tinge. Nickel is a hard and ductile transition metal. Pure nickel is chemically reactive, but large pieces are slow to react with air under standard conditions because a passivation layer of nickel oxide forms on the surface that prevents further corrosion. Even so, pure native nickel is found in Earth's crust only in tiny amounts, usually in ultramafic rocks, and in the interiors of larger nickel–iron meteorites that were not exposed to oxygen when outside Earth's atmosphere.

Global use of nickel is currently 68% in stainless steel, 10% in nonferrous alloys, 9% electroplating, 7% alloy steel, 3% foundries, and 4% other (including batteries).

Nickel is used in many recognizable industrial and consumer products, including stainless steel, alnico magnets, coinage, rechargeable batteries (e.g. Nickel–iron), electric guitar strings, microphone capsules, plating on plumbing fixtures, and special alloys such as permalloy, elinvar, and invar. It is used for plating and as a green tint in glass. Nickel is preeminently an alloy metal, and its chief use is in nickel steels and nickel cast irons, in which it typically increases the tensile strength, toughness, and elastic limit. It is widely used in many other alloys, including nickel brasses and bronzes and alloys with copper, chromium, aluminium, lead, cobalt, silver, and gold.

ABOUT DAVID GOMADZA

Visit www.twofuture.world

Introducing Nickel As The New Currency

Introducing Nickel As The New Currency

Introducing Nickel As The New Currency

Introducing Nickel As The New Currency

www.ingramcontent.com/pod-product-compliance
Lightning Source LLC
Chambersburg PA
CBHW031524210526
45464CB00007B/3020